For my
Patricia,
You dear woman!

TIMELESS NIGHT

Thank you for your
wisdom & spirit!

Love,

Elizabeth

M000110543

Also by Elizabeth Clark-Stern

Out of the Shadows
A Story of Toni Wolff and Emma Jung
ISBN 978-0981393940

On the Doorstep of the Castle
A play of Teresa of Avila and Alma de Leon
ISBN 978-1771690027

Soul Stories
Safari to Mara and Aria of the Horned Toad
ISBN 978-1926975009

TIMELESS NIGHT

Viktor Frankl meets Edith Stein

Elizabeth Clark-Stern

il piccolo editions
by

fisher king press

il piccolo editions by Fisher King Press
www.fisherkingpress.com
info@fisherkingpress.com
1-800-228-9316 Toll free Canada & the U.S.
+1-831-238-7799 International

Timeless Night
Copyright © 2014 Elizabeth Clark-Stern
ISBN 978-1-77169-019-5
First Edition

All rights reserved. No part of this book may be reproduced in any form or by any means, electronic or mechanical, including photocopying, recording, or by any information storage and retrieval system without permission in writing from the publisher.

Published simultaneously in Canada and the United States of America. For information on obtaining permission for use of material from this work, please submit a written request to:

permissions@fisherkingpress.com

Many thanks to all who have directly or indirectly provided permission to quote their works. Every effort has been made to trace all copyright holders; however, if any have been overlooked, the author will be pleased to make the necessary arrangements at the first opportunity.

Front cover image, Wren photo © John Stern 2014

ACKNOWLEDGMENTS

Many people gave their time and talents to make this book possible.

To Robert Bergman, our Viktor Frankl, for his suggestions and support and brilliance, and the lion tamer joke.

To Kevin Filocamo, for his directing notes that went far beyond the duties of a Stage Manager.

To Lindsey Rosen, Nancy Qualls-Corbett, and Donna Lee, for their enthusiasm and support.

To the C.G. Jung Society, Seattle, the Jungian Psychotherapist Association, and the Northwest Alliance for Psychoanalytic Study, for their undying support of the Shrink Wrap Theater Company.

Huge gratitude to Beverly Olevin and Susan Scott for their feedback and encouragement on the script.

To Lee Roloff for his inspiration and undying support through all the years.

And, as always, love and gratitude to my wonderful editor and publisher, Patty Cabanas and Mel Mathews.

For my beloved cousin, David Gooden, whose inspiration, support, courage, and love have provided a foundation for my development as a therapist, a writer, and a human being, for all these wonderful years.

And for my husband, John, whose humor, sensibility, and love echo through these pages, as they have for 35 years.

Timeless Night is a work of creative imagination based on historical figures Viktor Frankl and Edith Stein, and real events in their lives.

Timeless Night premiered on Feb. 1, 2014 at the Good Shepherd Chapel Theater in Seattle, Washington, a Shrink Wrap Theater Company workshop production sponsored by the Northwest Alliance for Psychoanalytic Study, the Seattle Jung Society, and the Jungian Psychotherapist Association.

Some sources of research used by the playwright:

Man's Search for Meaning, Recollections: An Autobiography, and *The Will to Meaning* by Viktor Frankl.

Finite and Eternal Being, Life in a Jewish Family, and *The Philosophy of Psychology and the Humanities* by Edith Stein.

And, *Edith Stein: The Life of a Philosopher and Carmelite* by Teresia Renata Posselt.

CHARACTERS IN ORDER OF APPEARANCE

Edith Stein, a woman of middle age (can be played by an actor age 40 on up)

Viktor Frankl, a man of middle age (can be played by an actor age 30 on up)

SETTING

A storeroom in Auschwitz

TIME

A spring night late in the Second World War

ORIGINAL CAST

Edith Stein	Elizabeth Clark-Stern
Viktor Frankl	Robert Bergman

CREW

Stage Manager	Kevin Filocamo
Lighting Design and Operation	John Stern

ARTISTIC CONSULTANT

Script Review and Feedback	Susan Scott

Lights fade up. A harsh white light illuminating the figure of Edith kneeling before a packing box, her head bowed in prayer. She wears a prison garment, her hair cropped, blood drying on her temple.

There is one other packing box in the otherwise empty room.

Off stage, the SOUND of a door opening. Slamming.

Edith breathes deeply. She does not open her eyes.

Viktor enters. He too wears prison garments.

Edith makes the sign of the cross; turns her body to face him.

EDITH:
> You've come to murder me.

VIKTOR:
> No. I'm a prisoner too.

EDITH:
> The Jews who do the dirty work for the SS, the so-called *capos*, they are prisoners.

VIKTOR:
> I am not a *capo*. I am a man.

EDITH:
> So you are.

> *They look upon one another.*

EDITH:
(continuing)

> The light, from the guard tower. So harsh.

VIKTOR:
> You prefer darkness?

EDITH:

It doesn't matter.

VIKTOR:

I prefer the light.

Silence.

VIKTOR:
(continuing)

There is blood on your face.

EDITH:

The SS man was forceful. Odd, since I offered no resistance.

VIKTOR:

I would tend your wound, but I have nothing on me that does not reek of the filth of Auschwitz.

EDITH:

You want to prevent infection?

VIKTOR:

I am a doctor.

EDITH:

I won't be here long enough for it to heal.

VIKTOR:

How do you know? They are unsettled. Can't you feel it?

EDITH:

You believe the stories. The Americans are coming.

VIKTOR:

All through the camp, whispers, shy ones, but with the mightiest hope.

EDITH:

Liberation...

VIKTOR:

They are beginning to *lose*.

EDITH:

Say that again.

VIKTOR:

The Germans, they are *losing*. We may survive this night.

EDITH:

You are an optimist.

VIKTOR:

You see the world as it is.

EDITH:

A realist. I was, once.

VIKTOR:

No longer?

EDITH:

Who knows what I am now? I was a philosopher, an atheist, searching for a truth that could be logically proven to all mankind.

VIKTOR:

Weren't you praying when I came in?

EDITH:

I was. I am. Even as I speak to you, another river in my mind whispers to God. It is quite rude. Forgive me.

VIKTOR:

Be my guest. I am fascinated that you can forage so many rivers at the same time. I was—I am—a psychiatrist.

EDITH:

A doctor of the mind.

VIKTOR:

Here I am only useful to them as a doctor of the body, in the typhus ward. I will keep my distance.

EDITH:

You suffer from the disease?

VIKTOR:

Not yet. I surely carry it.

EDITH:

You are not a leper, doctor, and I will die at dawn.

VIKTOR:

They told you this?

EDITH:

No, but they don't like troublemakers. My presence was so offensive to some in the women's barracks, they spit on me, clawed at me, screaming, "Traitor!" A Nazi soldier seized me from the arms of my sister, my Rosa. For some reason, she offended no one... They let me keep my eyeglasses, toy with me, cat and mouse. I thought they would shoot me on the spot. The SS man who roughly held me in his arms muttered, "It will not be me who pulls the trigger." I suspect he was once a good Catholic boy. I blessed him. He smacked me with his rifle butt and threw me in here.

VIKTOR:

You are Dr. Stein.

EDITH:

I was. I am now Sister Benedicta of the Cross. My Order sent Rosa and me to a convent in Holland for protection. Shortly afterwards, the monks there issued a public letter, condemning the Nazi persecution of the Jews. The Gestapo retaliated by rounding up all Catholics of Jewish descent.

VIKTOR:

I am so sorry.

EDITH:
(amazed, moved)

You are sorry...Many believe I became a nun to escape from the fate of my people. I would have the world know differently. It doesn't matter now.

VIKTOR:

I think it does.

EDITH:

Why? Of what use is this body? Does my soul live here?

VIKTOR:

You talk like you're already dead.

EDITH:

Of what possible value, these few remaining minutes?

VIKTOR:

They are our minutes. I'll take whatever I can get.

Edith turns away from him and returns to prayer.

Silence.

Viktor examines the other box, sits on it, studying her.

VIKTOR:
(continuing)

What does God say about all this?

EDITH:

Are you really interested?

VIKTOR:

Yes, Dr. Stein.

EDITH:

He tells me that the cross is being laid upon the Jewish people, and that most of them—

VIKTOR:

"Them?"

EDITH:

Us. Most of *us* do not understand this, but those who do must take up this cross on behalf of all. I offered myself to God for this purpose. Do I offend you?

VIKTOR:

You have three identities: atheist philosopher, Catholic nun, and Jew.

EDITH:

Which one is being executed?

VIKTOR:

If that is indeed your fate.

EDITH:

Alright. "If."

VIKTOR:

Then, only you know the answer.

EDITH:

Three days ago I would have said, "Sister Benedicta of the Cross." Now?...Everything changed when they put us on that train.

VIKTOR:

For me as well. I have been here two years, seven months, three days, and tonight. Nothing resembles the life I knew before. The man I was, he is standing off somewhere, watching the person I am becoming.

EDITH:

Who is that?

VIKTOR:

A man of contradictions, one part animal, thinking, even now: will I be in greater danger by association with her?...They might come in and spray us both with bullets.

Silence.

7

Edith cannot look at him.

VIKTOR:
(continuing)

> The animal in me thinks, "Should I bang on the door?
> Express the same disgust they showed toward you in
> the barracks? Demand they put me somewhere else?
> Anywhere but where you are."

Silence.

EDITH:

> Why don't you do it, if you believe it will save you.
> You do not have to babysit me in my final hours.

VIKTOR:

> Damn right I don't. You have God. How can I
> compete with him?

EDITH:

> You are free.

VIKTOR:

> Am I? That is the question.

> *Viktor moves about the room.*

VIKTOR:
(continuing)

> I am more than an animal. The human in me is grateful
> you are here. If this is to be my last night on earth, at
> least I will spend it with another soul, a woman, who
> looks on me with tender, astonished eyes.

Silence.

VIKTOR:
(continuing)

> You're thinking, "What did *he* do?—Perhaps I will get sprayed with bullets because he has murdered an officer, or something worse. Just because he's a psychiatrist, is no prescription for moral behavior!"

Edith cannot look at him.

VIKTOR:

> I'm right, aren't I?

She doesn't move.

VIKTOR:

> Don't worry. Nothing so dramatic, although here they kill you for sneezing in the wrong direction. There is a wood stove in the typhus ward. They caught me roasting pilfered potatoes. The SS man had a gun to my head, but the Nazi doctor said, "Please kill him later. I have no one to help me clean up the mess in the middle of the night."

EDITH:

> He saved you.

VIKTOR:

> I think this war was not of his choosing.

EDITH:

> He needs you. If typhus doesn't take your life, you will survive this war.

VIKTOR:

> Now who is the optimist?

EDITH:

Something in you is infectious.

He chuckles. She smiles.

VIKTOR:

You have wit!

(to the Heavens)

Thank you!

Edith smiles

Try this one: A stranger arrives in a Polish village with a large Jewish population.

EDITH:

Poland before the war.

VIKTOR:

Oh yes, when a Polish village was a place of simple struggles and common joys. So, this stranger is looking for a brothel—do I offend?

EDITH:

That depends. Is it funny?

VIKTOR:

Such pressure! If you will let me finish—

EDITH:

Please.

VIKTOR:

The stranger is looking for a brothel. Embarrassed to ask directly, he stops an old Jew on the street and asks him, "Where does the rabbi live?" The answer is,

"Over there, in the house painted green."—"What!" shouts the stranger, pretending to be shocked, "Such a famous rabbi and he lives in a brothel?"—The old Jew is horrified, "How can you say such a thing? The brothel is that red house, over there."[1]

Edith erupts in laughter. Viktor smiles.

EDITH:

Do you keep them laughing, in the typhus ward?

VIKTOR:

Sometimes. Even dying men scold me for bad jokes.

EDITH:

Humor, from the Latin, "to be human."

VIKTOR:

I like that. Do you suppose we can quell our animal natures, just for tonight, and be as human, as humorous, as we can?

EDITH:

I would like that.

VIKTOR:

Good. No more talk of extinction.

She does not respond.

VIKTOR:
(continuing)

Did you hear me, or were you talking to God?

EDITH:

Do you still have any?

VIKTOR:

Dignity?

EDITH:

No, pilfered potatoes.

VIKTOR:

You're hungry.

EDITH:

Yes, and, ever since they herded us into the cattle car, in the tiny snatches of sleep I claimed amid the feces and flesh, I dreamed of my mother's latkes.

VIKTOR:

...the smell, sizzling in oil.

EDITH:

She had the most exquisite way of making them: each potato trimmed in a perfect spiral. She used plenty of oil and cooked them very slowly. Not one ever burned.

Silence.

VIKTOR:

How long have you been here?

EDITH:

Two days, two nights, and tonight.

VIKTOR:

In the beginning, I didn't understand, about sleep. If another prisoner had a nightmare, I woke him up. Then I realized, even a nightmare is better than the horror of waking up *here*.

EDITH:

When you can sleep, what do you dream?

VIKTOR:

My wife's face…her tender kisses…the curve of her body lying next to me…her smile…the tips of her fingers touching my face…her hands, sliding around my waist as she whispers in my ear…We were deported together, along with my parents, my brother, my sister…When we got here, they separated us at once. In my dreams, I see her turning back to look at me, her eyes filled with such love…I don't wait for dreams. In the typhus ward, or marching back and forth from the barracks, at stolen moments in this waking death, I picture her face, summon her voice.

Edith does not pray. She is looking at Viktor.

VIKTOR:

(continuing)

That first day, when I arrived here, I had a first draft of a manuscript sewn into the lining of my coat. They barked, "Take off your clothes!" I begged. I struggled with them. They hit me with the butt of their rifles. They took my coat away, with the book inside it.

EDITH:

How devastating.

VIKTOR:

Actually, they did me a favor. It was a rough draft, some good ideas, but after being here, I realize it needs a page one re-write. I work on it, all the time, like your constant chit-chat with the Almighty.

EDITH:

Are you working on it, at this very moment?

VIKTOR:

Hah! Caught me with my pants down.

They laugh.

VIKTOR:
(continuing)

I carry it in my pockets, and write short hand notes on scraps of paper with the stub of a pencil a friend stole for me.

Silence.

VIKTOR:
(continuing)

Tell me a joke.

EDITH:

I don't know any. I could tell you a story.

VIKTOR:

A good one?

EDITH:

A happy one…It was a very fine day, when Mama opened her kitchen to me. "Edie," she said, "Today you are five." I cried, "I want to go to school like the others!" "Not yet, my little lemon cake. Today, I will teach you to make the latke." My little fingers could not hold the knife. She had so much patience, and I, so wanting to please her. I can see her in my mind: young, strong, long before the war and my choices etched rivers in her face.

14

VIKTOR:

> I can see my own Mama, her round face, her smile.

EDITH:

> We called it the "flour toss." While the latkes were cooking so slowly, Mama would make little balls of the dough and we would toss them at the squirrels out the kitchen window.

> *She demonstrates. He laughs.*

EDITH:
(continuing)

> The poor tortured creatures would duck, and then pounce on the dough balls and pop them in their cheeks. I would be bold and toss one at Mama, and she would toss one at me, then it was not just dough balls, but fists of flour. The others would come home from school and find us covered in white!

> *They laugh.*

VIKTOR:

> When a Frenchman leaves your house, he never says goodbye. When a Jew leaves, he says goodbye and never leaves!

> *They laugh even more.*

EDITH:

> I had this dreadful cousin. He talked our ears off, for hours!

VIKTOR:

> I had an aunt. What torture!...Ah, Dr. Stein, you

have brought me back to a time when torture was a tiresome relative. Thank you.

EDITH:

The American writer, Mark Twain, said, "the secret to humor is not joy but sorrow. There is no humor in Heaven."

VIKTOR:

He never met my aunt!

EDITH:

I think Twain got it wrong. I'll bet they laugh all day in heaven. When I get there, I will tell Gabriele your joke.

Edith's wild laughter dissolves into despair. From despair comes her rage.

EDITH:
(calling out the window)

You—out there in the dark—Who are you, to take away our joy?

VIKTOR:

Stop it!

EDITH:

Come for me now, cowards.

VIKTOR:

Quiet! You make trouble for us *both*.

EDITH:

Are you so terrified of an old woman?

Viktor restrains her. Edith beats him with her fists. He holds her firmly.

She beats him until she is exhausted.

She weeps. He holds her.

VIKTOR:

I felt it too, in the beginning. I was beaten a lot. I learned to lock away my rage, in a secret little chamber in my soul. Those who can't do that, die very quickly here.

Silence.

She pulls away from him.

EDITH:

Will you do me a favor?

VIKTOR:

If I can.

EDITH:

Do me the honor to show me your mind.

VIKTOR:

Only if you promise to show me yours.

EDITH:
(a smile)

Like children playing doctor.

Viktor chuckles, takes her hand and escorts her to one of the boxes, gesturing for her to sit. She does so.

EDITH:

You have not told me your name, doctor.

VIKTOR:

On the manuscript now ashes in a Nazi fire, it read, *The Doctor and the Soul*, by Viktor Frankl.

EDITH:

Perhaps they didn't burn it. Perhaps they are reading it, even as we speak. I recognized one of them as I got off the train. We were philosophy fellows together, at Gottingen.

VIKTOR:

—home of Europe's greatest journal of philosophy.

EDITH:

The *Jahrbuch*—I was its editor.

VIKTOR:

I'm embarrassed I didn't notice your name.

EDITH:

My authorship was not evident, though I did more than clarify the words of others. I slipped in some of my own original thought. I have been a writer, a teacher all my life, but I was denied a proper professorship. First because I am a woman, then because I am a Jew.

VIKTOR:

Your words opened my mind to the science of *being*. It changed the way I see the world.

EDITH:

Do you mean that?

VIKTOR:

Cracked opened my literal mind: "the poetry of direct experience is the source of all knowledge."

EDITH:

"...the poetry of direct experience is the source of all knowledge..." an exact quote. Dr. Frankl, how can you remember it so precisely?"

VIKTOR:

By being awake to our consciousness, we can come to know our own essence.

EDITH:

What an astonishing coincidence, to meet you, *here*.

VIKTOR:

Why, sister Benedicta? Aren't you a believer in Divine Providence?

EDITH:

I was. After coming here, it is difficult to believe anything. A shameful confession, but God knows this already, so it is hardly a shock to Him.

VIKTOR:

Your doubt?

EDITH:

Yes. Are you such a rock of faith?

VIKTOR:

I was an atheist for a while, as a young man. It may even have been the influence of your *Jahrbuch*, herding me to a rational analysis of what *is*. Then one night I was walking home, the moon a white scythe, casting a shadow on the leaves at my feet. I heard my inner oracle—[2]

EDITH:

> —your inner oracle?

VIKTOR:

> That's what I call it. A voice that comes, seemingly from nowhere. It said, "Viktor, in the womb of faith, there is room for doubt."

Silence.

VIKTOR:
(continuing)

> In the ancient teachings of the Jews, the mind of God is large enough to include all dualities: faith and doubt, good and evil, creation, destruction.

EDITH:

> Extermination, Liberation.

VIKTOR:

> Tonight we hold them both.

EDITH:

> My arms ache from the weight of it.

VIKTOR:
(beat, with a sly smile)

> A man is carrying an ox down the road. The rabbi walks past and says, "What are you doing, my son?" The man says, "The wheel of my cart broke. My ox has nothing to pull." "But why carry him?" asks the rabbi. The man answered, "Somebody had to pick up the burden!"

She laughs. He chuckles.

Silence.

VIKTOR:

When did it begin for you, Dr. Stein, this ruthlessness for truth?

EDITH:

Ruthlessness? As far back as I can remember.

VIKTOR:

Before the "flour toss?"

EDITH:

Yes. In my mother's garden, I watched people come and go. I wondered why some acted and believed one thing, others something entirely different. I asked Mama, "What is real?" She handed me peas to shuck. "Eating is not all that is real," I thought, there must be something in the world people don't know about. I called it the '*this–ness*'—if everyone knew about it, they wouldn't need to pretend the way the rabbi does when he comes and stuffs his face with Mama's latkes and puffs himself up like an old goose. People wouldn't make wars.

VIKTOR:

The wonder of your child mind.

EDITH:

When I was a teenager, I turned away from the rabbi and Mama's beloved Judaism. To my eyes, it was supernatural humbug.

VIKTOR:

How often we turn away from what we know.

EDITH:

> I wanted to find the underlying truth of our existence, a truth that would change the world.

VIKTOR:

> What does it mean for you now, *"this-ness?"*

EDITH:

> Our *being*. Not just who we are on the surface, but who we are as part of the substance of all things, now, and beyond time: *"this-ness."*

VIKTOR:

> You cannot simply say what it is, or name it.

EDITH:

> To give it academic language is to diminish it.

VIKTOR:

> You may remember that we Jews can never speak the name of God, for to do so makes Him a thing, and He is no thing. We have only the Hebrew letters, to symbolize He who is the Infinite, Always, Becoming.

> *Edith is disturbed by his words.*

EDITH:

> I am so sorry—I pulled your lecture into my own lap. Forgive me. Please, Dr. Frankl, share with me your re-write of *The Doctor and the Soul.*

> *He stares at her, turns away.*

VIKTOR:

> Would you speak my first name?

EDITH:

Why?

VIKTOR:

I'm curious, that's all.

EDITH:

Very well. "Viktor."

VIKTOR:

(closing his eyes)

It has been so long since I heard a woman's voice say my name. My mother was so loving, so pious, and I a "pest." She cradled me at night and sang a lullaby, "long, long ago—" She added her own lyrics, "Keep quiet you little pest, long, long ago—"

EDITH:

Your brain was restless.

VIKTOR:

No, Dr. Stein, I was a *pest*.

She smiles.

VIKTOR:

(continuing)

I loved my home so much, whenever I had to stay away, I was homesick. Even when I began working at various hospitals, I wanted to spend my nights at home.

EDITH:

There was laughter.

VIKTOR:

> Always. My mother lifted her skirts like a chorus girl, "I am your mama, but I can be naughty."

EDITH:

> Your mind grew, supping on simple joys.

VIKTOR:

> Like yours.

EDITH:

(looking away)

> Yes…like mine.

VIKTOR:

> My father was the penniless son of a bookbinder. He told stories of scraping potato peelings from a trash can. As a boy I judged him so harshly. He was so Spartan, so strict. My brother and I had to say our Hebrew just so, or he would punish us. Now, I scrape carrot peels out of the ice with my fingernails. I wish Papa were here, so I could tell him that I understand now, what it was like to be hungry, to live every day in fear. He will never know I have come to see his soul, to love his frown, his sigh after dinner at night, the way he looked out the window, wondering what was to come.

Viktor allows himself to feel.

VIKTOR:

(continuing)

> Shortly after we arrived here, I found my father dying of pulmonary edema and struggling for air as he neared death. I was able to steal a vial of morphine

and inject him with it to ease his suffering. "Do you have pain?" I asked him. "No," he whispered. "Do you have any wish?" "No." "Do you want to tell me anything?" "No." I kissed him and left. I knew I would not see him alive again, but that day, I had the most wonderful feeling one can imagine. I had done what I could. I had stayed in Vienna because of my parents, and I had accompanied him to the threshold and had spared him unnecessary agony in death.[3]

EDITH:

You had a chance to leave Vienna, and you did not go?

VIKTOR:

About a week before Pearl Harbor, I was granted a visa. I thought myself so fortunate—almost all of the Jews in Vienna had already been deported. As a doctor in a prestigious hospital, I was granted this last chance to get out. On my way to the American Consulate to pick it up, I hesitated. I knew what my parents' fate would be: deportation to a concentration camp. I walked for hours, and I had this thought: "Isn't this the kind of situation that requires some hint from heaven?" When I returned home, my eyes fell on a little piece of marble lying on the table. "What's this?" I asked my father. "This? Oh, I picked it out of the rubble of the synagogue they have burned down. It has on it part of the Ten Commandments. There is only one commandment that uses the letter that is chiseled here." "And that is…?" I asked eagerly. "Honor thy father and thy mother."[4]

Edith weeps.

VIKTOR:
(continuing)

> I'm sorry. I rattle on and on in tragedy. Our contract was for comedy.

EDITH:

> We have no contract, Dr. Frankl. Only *"this-ness…"*

VIKTOR:

> What can I say to bring you comfort in the bleakness of this starry night?

EDITH:

> Is it?

VIKTOR:

> Bleak?

EDITH:

> No, starry.

VIKTOR:

> Yes! I saw them in the typhus ward: a million twinkling magesties—

EDITH:
(glancing out the window)

> The light from the guard tower is too bright. It washes away the heavens.

VIKTOR:

> Close your eyes. You can see them—the Great Square of Pegasus, the Seven Sisters, lounging on the horizon—

EDITH:
(eyes closed "seeing")

The Pleiades.

VIKTOR:

Yes.

EDITH:

You're not making this up to make me feel better?

VIKTOR:

No. The Dipper. He was out too.

EDITH:

I don't think that's possible, not all those constellations on the same night.

VIKTOR:

You're wrong.

EDITH:

What does it matter?

VIKTOR:

It matters as nothing else has ever mattered in your life, in mine. *Here*, I notice everything in the natural world, as if I had never seen it before: every bud, every leaf, the moon—

EDITH:

In the train, on the way here—

VIKTOR:

—two nights ago.

EDITH:

Full, brilliant orange, big as a mountain—

VIKTOR:

—A harvest moon in spring!

EDITH:

I thought, "So shines the moon at the end of the world."

VIKTOR:

Or, the beginning.

EDITH:

Always such a positivist?

VIKTOR:

Once, when I was a boy, falling asleep in Mother's arms; she sang "Long, long ago little pest..." and I looked at the wrinkles on her hand and I thought, "She will die one day. I will die one day." I began to tremble. Mama held me tighter. What troubled me was not the fear of dying, but whether the transitory nature of life might destroy its meaning.[5]

EDITH:

Your little soul, seeing so much...

VIKTOR:

I have come to believe that it is death itself that makes life meaningful. All the losses along the way give us the opportunity to learn we can be stronger than we thought, take a new path, try a new skill, love again. We make a friend of our own free will, and create a life of beauty from the rubble, like pearls of great price on a golden chain. Nothing is ever lost.

EDITH:

Sentimental tripe, Dr. Frankl! *Everything* is lost for the Jews.

VIKTOR:

If it takes all night, I will convince you otherwise.

EDITH:

To find meaning, *here?*

VIKTOR:

Most particularly, *here.*

EDITH:

Your task is folly. I have one purpose: Christ has chosen me to be one of us who carries his cross for all Jews.

VIKTOR:

To atone for the sin of being Jewish?

EDITH:

No. If God had had the power to stop Hitler, He would have. History put this cross on the backs of our people, not God.

VIKTOR:

Sister Benedicta speaks with a very different voice than Dr. Stein.

EDITH:

As a philosopher, I was devoted to reason. As Sister Benedicta, I've come to see that rationality has its limits, but I still believe in the marriage of reason and faith.

VIKTOR:

Thomas Aquinas.

EDITH:

Yes. I stood on his shoulders, seeking to reconcile the two greatest forces in the human psyche.

VIKTOR:

I often say that about Freud. I stood on his shoulders, able to see a vast landscape that eluded him.

EDITH:

"Ambition doth or'leap itself."

VIKTOR:

Macbeth?

EDITH:

I think it was *Julius Caesar*—no matter. Ego, a fire I know quite well. I trotted into Gottingen hell bent on creating a new philosophy that would change the world. People would cry, "The truth, at last, and from a woman!"

VIKTOR:

You call it ego. You also had great courage.

EDITH:

No. Courage is something entirely different. But I was curious. I believed, even then, that scientific knowledge must include the spirit—the world we cannot see—

VIKTOR:

"There are more things in heaven and earth than are dreamt of in your philosophy."

EDITH:

Hamlet. My favorite play. I took my students every year.

VIKTOR:

"To be, or not to be." Shakespeare knew all about "*this-ness.*"

EDITH:

> What joy, Dr. Frankl, to watch your mind flash with light.

VIKTOR:

> A pleasure for me as well.

Silence.

VIKTOR:

> ...God has been re-constructing my mind since the day I arrived here. My ego was demolished when they confiscated my coat with my precious book. In it I had written my own definition of the nature of being! I fretted more about losing that book, than about what was happening to the people around me. I found another coat, threadbare, barely intact. In the pocket was a page probably torn from a prayer book on its way to a Nazi fire, the principal prayer of our people, *Sh'ma Yisrael, Adonai Eloheinu, Adonai Echad.*

EDITH AND VIKTOR:
(in unison)

> "Hear, oh Israel, the Lord our God. The Lord is One."

VIKTOR:

> In 1935, a Jew fired from his job is able to get work only as a lion tamer. On his first day at the circus, he goes into the cage and approaches the lion with a chair and a whip in his trembling hands. In terror he prays, *"Sh'ma Yisrael"*—*"Adonai Eloheinu,"* the lion says, "Do you think you're the only Jew out of work in Berlin?"

They erupt with laughter.

31

EDITH:

> Mama would have loved that joke. I close my eyes, I hear her voice, "*Sh'ma Yisrael, Adonai Eloheinu, Adonai Echad.*"

VIKTOR:

> In my home, it was Papa's voice, low barrel-chested, "*Sh'ma Yisrael, Adonai Eloheinu, Adonai Echad.*"

EDITH:

> My brother, Paul, sang it as he carried me around the house.

VIKTOR:

> You were the baby?

EDITH:

> I was so light, Paul must have thought me a toy. He sang to me, the rhymes of the day. We sang together…He is in America. Eventually, they all left except Mama, Rosa and me. My sister, Erna, her husband, my niece, Susel, the darling of my life, always far wiser than her young years. She knew my heart better than anyone in the family. We held each other, that last day, my chin resting on her soft brown hair.

> *Edith weeps.*

VIKTOR:

> You stayed behind because your mother could not get a visa to leave Germany?

EDITH:

> Doctor, please—

VIKTOR:

> I'm sorry.

EDITH:

(attempting to overcome great emotion)

> You may find this interesting, Dr. Frankl. In 1922, I wrote a book, *The Philosophy of Psychology and the Humanities.* It was my particular interest to encourage, indeed, to pioneer what you seem to have been working on all your life: the translation of philosophy's being-in-the-world, to the new field of psychology.

VIKTOR:

> Please excuse my interrogation of your past. I know you are grateful to have so many of your family safe, in America.

EDITH:

(in a quiet agony)

> Please. Read your scraps of paper to me.

VIKTOR:

(pulling scraps from his pocket, reading)

> "The study of *Being* - is an attempt to describe the way in which a man understands himself, in which he interprets his own existence, far from preconceived patterns of interpretation—"[6]

EDITH:

> —a dig at Freud.

VIKTOR:

> Precisely.

He watches as she struggles to contain her emotions.

EDITH:

> Dr. Frankl, I'm hardly a big fan of Freud, but theory

does help de-code one's childhood influences. Without it you are left with only curiosity and some poor patient's rambling.

VIKTOR:

Dr. Stein, you are suffering.

EDITH:

Please. Respond to my challenge, if you dare!

VIKTOR:

If you insist, Dr. Stein. You make a valid point. I simply resist an artificial template laid across anyone's "ramblings."

EDITH:

All constructs of the mind do so. Something is emphasized, something else, eliminated.

Edith sobs. Viktor reaches for her. She gestures for him to keep his distance.

EDITH:
(continuing)

Some of us deserve to suffer, Dr. Frankl. Wouldn't Freud say that?

VIKTOR:

No. I don't think so. His great passion was to create a psychology that would heal the deepest wounds of the psyche. He was so kind to me, printing my first essay in his journal, taking me under his wing. I wanted his approval. I wonder what he would have made, of this place?

EDITH:

They would have gassed him at once.

VIKTOR:

He did not want to leave Vienna. "I want to stay at my post," he said, ever loyal to his patients, holding tightly to his hard-won citadel of esteem among the anti-Semitism he had fought all his life. He was dying of cancer, so he knew he did not have long. At last he was persuaded to flee to London with his family.

EDITH:

He listened to the entreaty of other, wiser souls.

VIKTOR:

Freud lived and died in silken spaces. His couch, what fabric! I touched it once, when his back was turned. I was so silly, so in awe. Being here has shown me that psychotherapy must be more than mere technique. It must be the *encounter* of one human with another, an art that goes beyond pure science to wisdom.[7]

EDITH:

Do you practice your art here?

VIKTOR:

When I can. Two days ago I saw the body of a woman who had committed suicide. Among her effects there was a scrap of paper on which she had written, "More powerful than fate is the courage that bears it." Despite this motto, she had taken her life.[8]

EDITH:

She must have lost everyone she loved. Life was no longer worth living.

VIKTOR:

No, I don't believe that. As long as there is life, there is the possibility of meaning. If she had been stricken with typhus, she would have come to my clinic—

EDITH:

Your clinic?

VIKTOR:

Yes. *My* clinic. Where "fate" has put me. I could have talked with her, my soul touching hers, and from this, if she had been willing to find the jewels of hope and curiosity in her own inner being—

EDITH:

What if she could not find it?

VIKTOR:

You don't believe it's possible. But I have seen those few who do find something in themselves they have never seen before, and its light outshines death itself.

EDITH:

Did Freud find it?

VIKTOR:

I don't know. I hope so. He died in '39, in London.

EDITH:

All his family safe beside him?

VIKTOR:

No. His four sisters could not get out of Vienna.

EDITH:

Was he close to them?

VIKTOR:

Apparently. The youngest, Aldofina, his favorite from childhood. He carried her around, even as your brother carried you.

EDITH:

What happened?

VIKTOR:

He tried to get them out from London, writing to contacts, no doubt agonizing over it.

EDITH:

They never got out.

VIKTOR:

All four were exterminated…in a sister camp, not far from here.

Silence.

VIKTOR:
(continuing)

Freud did not know. He died before they were deported.

EDITH:

He must have suspected, "known" in his heart.

VIKTOR:

Perhaps.

EDITH:

Mama died before this happened to Rosa and me… She too must have "known." God is there deep inside. Your "inner oracle." But what could she have done? All was lost.

Edith expresses her despair.

VIKTOR:

I'm sorry. I have been here long enough to build walls of flaming stone around my heart. I forget—as Shakespeare said, "Tis new to thee."

EDITH:

Miranda. *The Tempest.* A girl, alone on an island with her father.

VIKTOR:

(taking her hand, ushering her back to sit on a box)

Come with me, Dr. Stein, back to the lifeboat of theory. Laced into the foundation of Freud's analysis, there is a reduction in the possibilities for meaning. Even in his interpretation of dreams, a slicing to the core, but only as he defined the core. I came to feel there was not enough room for the core of me, or the core of the patient.

EDITH:

You criticize him, yet, you love him.

VIKTOR:

I revere him. I owe him.

EDITH:

You love him.

Silence.

VIKTOR:

I love him.

EDITH:

>This love allows you to forgive his rigidity, his blind spots. What if his transgressions were horrible, like those men out there in the dark with the twisted crosses on their sleeves?

Silence.

VIKTOR:

>Is there someone you are struggling to forgive?

Silence.

>*Viktor observes her. She will not look at him as she prowls around the room, like a caged beast. He follows her movements.*

EDITH:

>Continue your lecture, Dr. Frankl.

Silence.

EDITH:
(continuing)

>Please.

VIKTOR:

>I am more interested in the theme you have introduced.

EDITH:

>No. I cannot breathe with your eyes upon my heart.

VIKTOR:

>Do you need a joke?

EDITH:

> Sure.

Silence.

VIKTOR:

> I can't think of one. I'm sorry.
>
> *Edith paces until she can do it no more. She curls onto a box. Viktor watches her.*

EDITH:

> Help me. Ask me about my work.

Silence.

VIKTOR:

> Alright, give me a real world example of your philosophy of Being.

EDITH:

> Thank you.
>
> *Breathing, searching her thoughts.*
>
> My mind betrays me…To answer you, I must return to the last place I want to go: Mama. Her anise cookie. Right before Hanukkah, she rolled out the dough and I had the honor to stamp the little drummer boy in the center. The whole kitchen smelled of the licorice-scented herb.

VIKTOR:
(eyes closed)

> "Long, long ago…little pest…"

Silence.

They close their eyes, breathing in the scents of childhood.

EDITH:

> Mama never used a recipe. If it had not been for her creativity, the anise cookies would have remained inert flour, sugar, and neglected bits of dried anise.

VIKTOR:

> Her love made the cookies come into being.

EDITH:

> In my family, I never questioned what I experienced as love. It was later that I struggled with it, as a woman, feeling I should love some man, and what exactly was "love?" My father died when I was two. I have no memories of him. Perhaps Freud would make hay of that.

VIKTOR:

> What would you make of that?

EDITH:

> I don't know. I have no inner image of "father," or of my parents together. I cannot speak to what was never there.

Silence.

EDITH:
(continuing)

> It is important to me to tell you of my first real love. I don't know why...Perhaps your essence here, this night is teaching me that I don't have to justify everything. I can just feel this longing, to tell you, and let it just be...It was twenty years ago. I was thirty, but still such a girl. I went to the country home of dear

41

friends, to rest, to be with them. They went shopping in town, leaving me to the blessed solitude of their library. On the shelf, a worn copy of the autobiography of a Saint I had vaguely heard of, a trouble-maker in her day, who wrote of her discourse with God. In my staunch atheist days, I would never have given it the time of day, but that morning, nourished perhaps by the gentle spirit of my friends—

VIKTOR:

—nothing is lost.

EDITH:

I pulled the book off the shelf. It was as if a part of me had been sitting in the center of a garden in my soul, waiting. This part of me had watched the rest of me plough through scores of texts on philosophy, then to write my *own*. I made up my own term to describe the motivations of man. "Lifepower" I wrote that in 1916, before I was aware of Freud and his "libido."

VIKTOR:

"Lifepower…"

EDITH:

That which comes from deep within and gives meaning to our conscious choices. If you are unconscious of your Lifepower, you knock about, attempting to please others, searching for esteem in idle pursuits that go nowhere.

VIKTOR:

The essence within.

EDITH:

Yes, I now see that it was my Lifepower that guided

me to reach for the Saint's autobiography that fateful day. I knew there was something lacking in my life, a way of being, not only in the world, but in *myself*, that has so far eluded me. I read the Saint's rambling, often giddy text, a stream of consciousness by an unschooled, cloistered nun from 16th century Spain.

VIKTOR:

Not a scholar.

EDITH:

No, and hence the brilliance of its author: Teresa of Avila. I could feel it in every phrase—her Lifepower. Raw, unedited, repetitive…real.

She settles in stillness.

EDITH:
(continuing)

I read it straight through. It was raining, a warm, late afternoon cloudburst. I walked through the streets, into the fields beyond. This other Edith inside me, who had been waiting in my inner garden for thirty years, leapt up and joined me at last. We ran through the rain. It was as if I held her hand, felt the warmth and joy of her being coming alive in me. Suddenly my only ambition was to come into my true being: a woman in love with God. No one was more surprised than I.

Silence.

VIKTOR:

Thank you.

EDITH:

Can you understand?

VIKTOR:

Of course. You speak of your love for God with all the passion of Juliet for her Romeo.

EDITH:

Hopefully a more mature love, but yes, there was the quality of being a young girl, consumed with passion.

Silence.

VIKTOR:

Her name is Tilly. My wife. I saw her, that first day, walking in the hospital corridor. I gasped. Even dressed in a gray nursing smock, she moved with the elegance of a Spanish dancer. The way her arm settled on a tray, the tilt of her head as she glanced up at me. "Where are your castanets?" I asked. She laughed. I detected a blush in the high trill of her laugh, then a trace of the bawdy, as if, this one woman contained all that was innocent and deliciously worldly. I did not marry her for her beauty, or even her wonderful laughter. I married her for her character, demonstrated in a thousand subtle acts of kindness and a depth of discernment that taught me, that continues to teach me.

Silence.

VIKTOR:
(continuing)

Here, even as the image of her face keeps me alive, I curse the pain that floods over me in the night, the

44

fear, at times the certainty, that she is dead. I can't bear to think I will never hold her close again, or see her face looking at me with such love.

He weeps.

EDITH:

Surely they have put her to use here as a nurse.

VIKTOR:

I do not make meaning of suffering by concocting a soothing fairy tale.

He weeps. Edith observes him closely.

VIKTOR:

(continuing)

I tend my despair as if holding a child, rocking him, reminding him that we do not know the future.

Silence.

She goes to him. Reaches out to touch him. Backs away.

EDITH:

Dr. Frankl, I just remembered something. May I tell you now, for if I don't, I'm afraid I won't remember it, and it will be lost.

VIKTOR:

We do not want more loss, do we?

EDITH:

No. A man is sent to a psychoanalyst because he suffers from headaches, congestion in the head, and ringing in his ears—and the analyst will undoubtedly

45

find many deep, unconscious causes for these symptoms. On his way to the appointment, however, the man passes a clothing store and remembers that he needs a new shirt. He enters and asks for a certain brand. "What size?" asks the sales clerk. "Fifteen," is the answer. "I'm sure you need at least a 16." "Give me a 15," says our man, "and no questions." "Okay, but don't be surprised if you suffer from headaches, congestion in the head, and ringing in the ears."[9]

Viktor chuckles. Edith is quite pleased with herself.

VIKTOR:

You have been holding out on me, Dr. Stein.

EDITH:

No! I remembered it, just now!

VIKTOR:

This is what I call "pure coincidence," our meeting here—behind the apparent coincidence a higher, or deeper ultimate meaning may be hidden. Not the fact that you wrote the *Jahrbuch* but that you showed up here to tell me that silly joke.

They laugh. He breathes.

VIKTOR:
(continuing)

Can you hear them, out there, pacing in the night?

EDITH:

Restless, as you said. Losing, as you said.

VIKTOR:

They pass this shed and hear our laughter.

EDITH:

They think we have gone mad.

VIKTOR:

We know something they don't.

EDITH:

They cannot know our secrets.

VIKTOR:

The home of joy inside us.

EDITH:

The love we feel for the soil of our homeland, even the soil, beneath this death camp.

Viktor looks at her curiously.

EDITH:

I was born a few miles north of here, in a town called Breslau. At my birth, this country we now call "Poland" was part of Germany. As a child, I ran in the countryside, climbed trees so I could look out upon this place I loved so well.

VIKTOR:

And so I love Austria. Every wildflower in the mountains, every cobblestone in Vienna.

EDITH:

On the train coming here, I peered through the boards of the cattle car. There it was: my countryside in spring, as beautiful as it had been in my youth. The last stop before Auschwitz, was Breslau...my Breslau.

VIKTOR:

> The train that carried us here stopped in my hometown, outside Vienna. It looked, remarkably the same.

EDITH:

> When my sister Erna was leaving for America, my niece, my Susel, cried out to me, her wise eyes so wet: "Edith, what are you doing? Come with us."—"No," I said, "I can never leave Germany!" Once I said it aloud, Rosa, Mama…they never considered leaving either…I knew the behavior of the Third Reich. I knew what was coming, but once I pledged my allegiance to my beloved homeland, a cloud settled over my mind. I lost the will to do what was in my heart—to run to my darling Susel, scoop her into my arms and shout, "Take me with you!" "Take Mama!" "Take Rosa!"

> *She weeps bitterly.*

EDITH:
(continuing)

> Rosa is here because of me.

VIKTOR:

> Can we judge ourselves, for this spring-load in our brain that obscures truth, rational action, Lifepower?

EDITH:

> You skewer me with my own word! Yes, we must judge ourselves, and the world. My cloud-mind, my denial, rationalizing, all this mental garbage determined my *actions.*

VIKTOR:

> Should we hate ourselves for what we could not see?

48

EDITH:

(looking out the window)

> We hate *them*? Didn't Hitler unleash a "cloud" over
> our entire, country? What of the dark corridors in
> his mind?

VIKTOR:

> I tremble to imagine it.

EDITH:

> You tremble, and turn away, in your zeal to make all
> men—and women—redeemable.

VIKTOR:

> I do not turn away. You put words in my mouth and
> motives in my soul. Blatant distortions. I have tilled
> this ground over and over in my mind every day for
> two years, seven months and three days: do they
> "know" what they are doing? Where does pathology
> end, and evil begin?

EDITH:

> Psychology proposes a theory of mind that is a-moral;
> ultimately incomplete. Philosophy requires ethical
> free will: we are responsible for our actions, clouds
> or no clouds—

VIKTOR:

> —there can be no free will to someone ensnared in
> low self worth, delusion——

EDITH:

> I made *choices* from this delusion. I was blind until I
> arrived *here*. This horror stripped the last shred of
> illusion from my eyes. It was too late. Am not evil?

VIKTOR:

> In the Torah, God holds us responsible, even for our clouds but, is that the whole truth?

EDITH:

> You put psychology above God?

VIKTOR:

> No. I believe God wants us to use all of our minds, and, when possible, refine his teachings. And, He also believes every soul is redeemable.

EDITH:

> I don't have to do this. I am not arguing a case in court.

VIKTOR:

> Oh yes you are. Both of us stand, this night, in the court of history. You harp on your "evil" as if there are no subtleties, no gray.

EDITH:

> You want me to forgive myself, though it does a violence to my own sense of justice.

VIKTOR:

> I would have you see the complexity of motivation, in yourself, in others.

EDITH:

> Enough. I am too hungry to argue.

> *She curls onto a box, exhausted.*

VIKTOR:

> One must never let hunger *win.*

EDITH:

Summon energy, no matter what?

VIKTOR:

Yes. Your word: Lifepower.

EDITH:

(a groan of ironic humor)

I should never have told you.

They laugh gently together.

VIKTOR:

An SS man shares a train compartment with a Jew. The Jew unpacks a herring, eats it, then wraps the head carefully and puts it in his pocket. The SS man asks why he is doing this. "The head of the fish contains the brain. I bring it home to my children, so that they will become smart." "How much will you take for the head?" asks the guard.

"One mark." "Here is your mark," says the SS man, and he eats the fish head. Five minutes later he goes into a rage. "You damn crook! The whole fish costs only half a mark, and you charged me a mark just for the head!" "See?" said the Jew, "It's beginning to work already."[10]

Edith laughs and laughs. Viktor smiles, watching her.

VIKTOR:

The Nazi doctor who saved my life tonight told me that joke. I suspect he had no choice but to accept his job in this camp. They are punishing him for something. He must be one of the Germans who helped the Jews escape early in the war.

51

Silence.

VIKTOR:
(continuing)

>Freud would say, "Viktor, that is projection!"

EDITH:

>He scolded you like a father.

VIKTOR:

>Affectionately. He said, "The cure, my boy, is love."

Silence.

EDITH:

>Mama refuses to come to me in my dreams. I beg God to send her. He is holding her close, protecting her from me...I lied to you, Dr. Frankl. It was not only that I would not leave my country. There is something much worse...The day before I left Mama forever to join the Order, we took a walk. "I'm sure your Jesus was a very nice man," she said, "but did he have to call himself a *God?*" Then she wailed. She knew it was my own selfishness that made it all happen. I had been offered a teaching position in America. I could have brought Rosa and Mama with me. But, no, I had fallen in love with God. I put that above my family.

>...When Mama was dying, Rosa came to the convent. I told her as a cloistered nun, they would not let me leave the convent. I belonged to God, not our family. Mama died. I was not there...I was not *there*. *(glancing at him)* You did not abandon your mama, your papa.

VIKTOR:

>No, I did not.

EDITH:

Say it: you would not leave them.

VIKTOR:

I was blessed not to be captured by that particular
cloud.

EDITH:

"Blessed?" You are a more moral man than me. Say
it.

VIKTOR:

You have no idea, woman. For two years, seven
months and three days, I watched the animal in me
come out. This very day I thought the man in front
of me would die. "Good," I thought. He has a crust
of bread in his pocket. I will steal it before anyone
else. I thought of Tilly, what they're doing to her, a
beautiful woman, if she is still alive. I thought of all
the ways I could sneak into the SS quarters and burn
it to the ground, murdering all of them. I saw what
I am capable of. It is as dark, as the greatest evil on
earth.

EDITH:

These are fantasies. You did not do it, Dr. Frankl.
There is a strength of character in you that has such
force, it overcomes all your murderous desires. That
is how good conquers evil.

VIKTOR:

And what determines, which of us has so strong a
Lifepower, and who doesn't? Who deserves guilt and
who doesn't? God? Chemistry? Wild chance? What if
we do not know? More importantly: what if it does
not matter? We are human beings, in this primordial
soup, tasked not to dispense justice, but to dispense

love. This guilt you are so proud of, that you hold to your breast like a precious jewel. What if you could toss it out? Who would be left, Edith? Who would you be, if you were guiltless?

EDITH:

A precious child, beloved of God.

VIKTOR:

You would be a precious child, beloved of your self. That is much harder, much closer to home.

She studies his face.

EDITH:

You scold me, like a husband.

VIKTOR:

You bring out the best in me.

EDITH:

What a surprise. In these final hours, I realize there is something I have missed. Something that may have kept me in line—confronted the false notes in myself years ago.

VIKTOR:

What? You want me to guess?

She smiles.

VIKTOR:

If you had become a piano tuner?

She shakes her head "no."

VIKTOR:

A comedienne?

EDITH:

No.

VIKTOR:

A high-wire aerialist?

EDITH:

Stop it. You know.

VIKTOR:

Marriage, to a mortal.

EDITH:

Top marks. I would have had my "truth" forever challenged. You will not let me hate myself, no matter how determined I am to do so.

VIKTOR:

Sorry, I meant to let you hate yourself, but I forgot.

EDITH:

Why do you *care*?

VIKTOR:

A good question. This is all a surprise to me too...I don't know. Being here with you tonight, holding you earlier, feeling the softness of your body, the tension of your mind. I couldn't resist taking it on.

EDITH:

No one has ever treated me like a wife before.

VIKTOR:

No one has ever *dared*.

EDITH:

> When Papa died, Mama had bourn eleven children; seven of us survived. She turned all her attention to the lumber business, taking over right where Papa left off. She never re-married. I never saw *this* growing up.

VIKTOR:

> You think it would have made a difference?

EDITH:

> Who knows? I have a hunch it might have given me an inner "Papa touchstone." Let's say I had it, this ease with finding a mate, and we were 20 year olds together.

VIKTOR:

> At university—

EDITH:

> —It is spring, lilac buds heavy on green branches—

VIKTOR:

> —You, sitting on the rim of the fountain, books on your lap, a pencil in your hair.

EDITH:

> —You walk by with your fellows. I see your eyes check out my legs.

VIKTOR:

> How did you know!

EDITH:

> You walk up to me and say, "Those books look dreadfully heavy, young lady—"

VIKTOR:

Oh, God. Give me a better line than that.

EDITH:

So. What?

VIKTOR:

I was always a terrible bungler. I would have been so flustered, by the sight of your legs, your ankles in brown socks, those dreadful Oxfords covering my imagination's etching of your toes...

EDITH:

Men really think of such things?

VIKTOR:

You have no idea. I would have walked past you, glancing back once to see if you looked on me at all.

EDITH:

Say I did. Say that when I saw you, this Papa touchstone clicked in my subconscious. I didn't know it then, but we would be married within the year, nurse one another through our doctorates, have three kids...

VIKTOR:

Two boys, one girl.

EDITH:

Two girls, one boy. After they grow up, it is you who become restless.

VIKTOR:

—weary of trundling about after you on all those book tours.

EDITH:

You have book tours of your own.

VIKTOR:

> They aren't as much fun as yours. But, yes, let's say I decide I have lost my self in your glory, and I go off to Africa with some chums.

EDITH:

> To shoot pictures, not animals.

VIKTOR:

> Of course. And you would come down, join the rough men on safari.

EDITH:

> I had to. I couldn't live without your bad jokes.

VIKTOR:

> And I missed turning you around whenever you tried to hate yourself.

EDITH:

> You missed that, even on safari?

VIKTOR:

> Of course. I missed the "all" of you.

EDITH:

> And, I would have been a different woman than I am now. It wouldn't have been all up to me, the decisions. I'd have seen your face at every turn, staring back at me, saying, "What do you mean we're not going to America!"

Edith crumbles. Viktor watches her struggle.

VIKTOR:

> Please, Dr. Stein——

EDITH:

(facing him bravely)

> Dr. Frankl, my wild tangential mind has taken us far afield. Please, tell me about your book.

VIKTOR:

(beat)

> If you insist, Dr. Stein.

> *Viktor goes to a box, spreads out his shards of paper, embracing the formality of a lecture hall.*

VIKTOR:

> It gets written every morning. I wake and feel the stench and death around me, and I think, "What new chapter can I begin today? Ah, The Will to Meaning!"

> *Edith weeps.*

VIKTOR:

> Don't weep for me.

EDITH:

> Don't tell me what to feel! I weep not for your demise, but for the beauty of your ideas...May I tell you something?

VIKTOR:

> Of course. Thank you for asking. You are learning to be a good "wife."

EDITH:

> I just wanted you to know, that in my doctoral dissertation, "*On the Problem of Empathy*—"

VIKTOR:

Problem? Without it, the art of psychotherapy is lost!

EDITH:

Please, "dear—"

VIKTOR:

Sorry. Continue, "dear."

EDITH:

Thank you. The "problem" was a limitation in the definition of Being. Before my dissertation, it had not been articulated that every soul needs reflection. Someone to empathize with us. What I saw in the eyes of my wise Susel, what I gave to her when I said, "You are an old soul, my love…" Without this reflection, we do not emerge complete, into the world. A cello sitting in the corner un-played, is not a "cello."

Ah—I did it again! Forgive me. Back to *your* book. More. Please, tell me more.

VIKTOR:

Nothing is ever lost. The past writes its own story, and we must trust that all we have been, all we have said, all whom we have loved, will find its home in the memory of the human world.

EDITH:

What guides this search for meaning?

VIKTOR:

Conscience.

EDITH:

What you have that I did not.

VIKTOR:

> Stop it, Dr. Stein. Conscience is not infallible. If you are guilty of anything, it is your cowardice now to stand up to your own self.

EDITH:

> My head spins.

VIKTOR:

> Sorry. I pre-empt myself. Please, get up.

Edith stands. Victor places one box, then another, making a triangle with Edith's own body.

VIKTOR:

(introducing each concept as a box, with Edith the third one)

> The three ways of manifesting meaning: 1.Creativity in the world.

EDITH:

> Mama's anise cookies.

VIKTOR:

> Exactly! 2. Experience—I come into the kitchen and eat her cookie—

EDITH:

> I can taste it.

VIKTOR:

> Ummm. So can I. And, finally, and most importantly, 3. Attitude.

EDITH:

> Why most important?

VIKTOR:

It is the one we have most control over at any given moment. We are limited by our gifts, or lack of them; by social class, by environment, but each of us, to our last conscious breath, has a choice of our attitude. Do we choose despair, or meaning?

EDITH:

What if we are mired in a despair we cannot climb out of—because of a great defect in our character?

VIKTOR:

There is one more triangle.

EDITH:

I hope this is clearer to your readers!

VIKTOR:

(shifting the boxes and her body to make a new triangle)

Tonight, I care only that it is clear, to you. From Attitude, we trace a final triangle, 1. Pain.

(he touches one box)

2. Death

(he touches the other)

3. Guilt.

(he gently touches Edith's shoulder)

EDITH:

Tag: you're it.

VIKTOR:

> In pain, one must take a stand against it, doing everything possible to alleviate suffering. In death, one must see it clearly and stand in grace. In guilt, one must take a stand to one's self. To be guilty is a privilege of mankind, for then, we can take responsibility. Can you stand—not before God, but before yourself, and say: I am guilty—I will make meaning of this.

EDITH:

> Now, tonight?

VIKTOR:

> There may be no other time, for either of us.

EDITH:

> Interesting, to hear you admit that, at last.

VIKTOR:

> What moral action are you guilty of?

EDITH:

> Moral action? You mean what have I done, not what did I fail to do?

VIKTOR:

> Yes.

EDITH:

> What actions, from my goodness?

VIKTOR:

> Yes. What you are proud of.

EDITH:

> After I entered the Order, I wrote a letter to the Pope, denouncing his collusion with the Nazi's in the deportation of the Jews from Italy. I begged for an

audience with him. It was denied. He continued his collusion, but the letter became known and unmasked a great hypocrisy.

VIKTOR:

What else?

EDITH:

When the Nazi's took us from the convent, I had almost completed a book, *Life in a Jewish Family*, the story of Mama, of all of us. I wanted to show the world the Jews are good people, who love their families. No different from other Germans, from any human creatures.

VIKTOR:

What else?

EDITH:

I fought for the rights of women, made it clear we are separate, valuable, independent human beings.

VIKTOR:

This did not make you popular.

EDITH:

I didn't care. I wanted other women to be granted professorships and power that I was denied.

VIKTOR:

What else?

EDITH:

I translated Thomas Aquinas's greatest work. My book, *Finite and Eternal Being*, integrated the philosophy of being with Aquinas's rational faith.

VIKTOR:

> I hope I live to read it.

EDITH:

> My body of work is unfinished. I will not live to write what I have learned *here*.

> *Viktor takes her hand.*

VIKTOR:

> Come.

> *She takes his hand. He leads her to the window, the harsh light pouring in from the guard tower.*

VIKTOR:
(continuing)

> I will be your witness. Who else do you want to hear your final statement on the truth of our finite and eternal being?

EDITH:

> My dearest Lord Christ.

VIKTOR:

> Who else?

EDITH:

> ...my mother.

VIKTOR:

> Tell her.

EDITH:

> Mama, I'm sorry. Forgive me for what I could not see. Always you said, "Edie, what have you learned?"...

Being here, I have learned, God is not enough. He too trembles in the face of this evil that boils away all semblance of who we once were. And what is left? What I have searched for all my life: the *experience* of the underlying *this-ness* of all existence, at once timeless, and *here*, alive, inside of us.

Viktor studies her face, turns away.

EDITH:

What is it?

VIKTOR:

I can't say.

EDITH:

Why not?

VIKTOR:

If I confess it, I promise not to act on it, like an un-played cello sitting in the corner.

EDITH:

What can it be, that you feel so strongly, yet cannot pluck?

VIKTOR:

(turning to face her)

Desire.

EDITH:

For an old nun?

VIKTOR:

For the woman standing before me.

EDITH:

> How extraordinary.

VIKTOR:

> Isn't it? To feel it, *here*, in spite of all they have done to destroy our "Lifepower."

EDITH:

> I feel it too, flowing between us, throughout this night.

VIKTOR:

> Your God is jealous.

EDITH:

> I don't think so. Is your wife?

VIKTOR:

> She would more than understand.

EDITH:

> No guilt?

VIKTOR:
(he smiles)

> I have a gift for you.

> *He produces a crisply burnt potato from his pocket.*

EDITH:

> A pilfered potato!

> *He offers it to her. She takes a ravenous bite, offers it to him. He takes a bite. They gobble it down, laughing, looking into each other's eyes.*

EDITH:

> We could escape together.

VIKTOR:

> Run away into the forest.

EDITH:

> Never be heard from again.

VIKTOR:

> History would say we died in the gas chambers.

EDITH:

> Years later we would be discovered in Brazil—

VIKTOR:

> —playing in a string quartet!

The light shuts OFF from the guard tower, replaced by a pale pink glow.

EDITH:

> Dawn...

She trembles.

EDITH:

> Could I ask you—could you hold me?

He curls his arms around her, his cheek resting against her hair.

EDITH:
(continuing)

> I intended to be brave.

VIKTOR:

> We can only *be*.

EDITH:

> My spirit is ready to meet God. My flesh trembles to
> imagine such a death.

VIKTOR:

> My flesh trembles to imagine the surprise on the faces
> of the American soldiers, "Hey, Joe, got a couple of
> live ones in here!"

EDITH:

> You make me laugh, even at the gates of death. How
> do you manage it?

> *Victor holds her closer.*

EDITH:
(continuing)

> Your very bones shiver...

VIKTOR:

> I am a great phony, Edith.

EDITH:

> Viktor. You are afraid.

VIKTOR:

> I have composed a speech, every day, for one year,
> seven months, three days, and tonight. If they come
> for me, and point me toward the gas chamber, I will
> lift my chest and say, "You can starve us, beat us,
> murder our bodies, you cannot take our *souls*, Edith's,
> mine, all of us—our free will, our laughter, our love,
> shining this night and for all eternity!"

EDITH:

A beautiful speech.

Viktor kisses her. She responds.

Off stage SOUND of the door opening.

Edith breathes quickly. Viktor holds her.

EDITH:

There is someone at the door.

They look upon one another.

EDITH:
(continuing)

Viktor, dear.

VIKTOR:

Yes, dear.

They embrace.

Silence fills the empty room.

Fade to black.

NOTES FROM HISTORY

In August of 1942, Edith Stein and her sister Rosa Stein were deported from their convent in Eck, Holland to Auschwitz. Although most accounts place their execution around August 9, some accounts speculate they may have not been executed until September 20 of that same year. Viktor Frankl was deported to Auschwitz with his parents, wife and sister in mid-September, 1942. This play takes place in the imaginal space where they could have met, in that slender window of time.

Edith and Rosa Stein were executed in 1942. Edith Stein's many books have been published by the Institute of Carmelite Studies, and translated into many languages. Biographies and films tell her story, and she was canonized as Saint Teresa Benedicta of the Cross in 1998 by Pope John Paul II. Her sainthood remains controversial among some Catholics, who believe she died because she was Jewish, not because she was a Catholic martyr.

Viktor Frankl survived the war and went on to write *Man's Search for Meaning*, the story of his experiences in the concentration camps, and the foundation of Logotherapy. Translated into many languages, the book has been a best-seller worldwide since its publication in the 1950's. Frankl went on to teach and lecture around the world, and to write many other books. He died in 1997.

A note on the casting: Viktor Frankl was 37 in 1942, Edith Stein was 50. However, since the play takes place in imaginal time and space, this opens possibilities for casting actors from a broad range of ages. Our original production featured actors much older than their historical counterparts, and this served to portray the archetypes of the wise old man and the wise old woman. Possibilities abound.

NOTES

The following notes record specific passages from Frankl's writing cited in the dialogue. It seems particularly important to make note of the jokes. No doubt he was not the original author of these jokes, but they are part of the life of humor and folklore that was an integral part of his character.

The rest of the dialogue is a translation, by the playwright, of what these people could have said, given the creative conceit of the play.

"Lifepower" is indeed a word coined by Edith, in 1916. For more information on her work, go to her books cited in the bibliography following the notes:

1. "The stranger is looking for a brothel...The brothel is that red house, over there." Viktor Frankl, *Recollections: An Autobiography*. Basic Books, 2000.

2. "inner oracle," Viktor Frankl, *Recollections: An Autobiography*. Basic Books, 2000.

3. "My father was the penniless son of a bookbinder... spared him unnecessary agony in death." Viktor Frankl, *Recollections: An Autobiography*. Basic Books, 2000.

4. "About a week before Pearl Harbor...Honor thy father and thy mother." Viktor Frankl, *Recollections: An Autobiography*. Basic Books, 2000.

5. "Once when I was a boy...might destroy its meaning." Viktor Frankl, *Recollections: An Autobiography*. Basic Books, 2000.

6. "The study of Being...patterns of interpretation."

Viktor Frankl, *The Will to Meaning: Foundations and Applications of Logotherapy*. Meridian Books, division of Penguin Books, 1969.

7. "It (psychotherapy) must be the encounter of one human with another, an art that goes beyond pure science to wisdom." Viktor Frankl, *The Will to Meaning: Foundations and Applications of Logotherapy*. Meridian Books, division of Penguin Books, 1969.

8. "Two days ago I saw the body...she had taken her life." Viktor Frankl, *Man's Search for Meaning*. Simon and Schuster, 1959.

9. "A man is sent to a psychoanalyst...ringing in the ears." Viktor Frankl, *Recollections: An Autobiography*. Basic Books, 2000.

10. "A man shares a compartment with a Jew...beginning to work already." Viktor Frankl, *Recollections: An Autobiography*. Basic Books, 2000.

BIBLIOGRAPHY

Meszaros, Marta (2010) *Edith Stein: The Seventh Chamber*, a film by Marta Meszaros. Written by Roberta Mazzoni and Marta Eva Palki. Ignatius Press films

Posselt, Teresia Renata (2005), *Edith Stein: The Life of a Philosopher and Carmelite*. Washington DC ICS Publications.

Stein, Edith (1986) *Life in a Jewish Family: Her Unfinished Autobiographical Account*. Washington DC ICS Publications.

Stein, Edith (2000) *The Philosophy of Psychology and the Humanities*. Washington DC ICS Publications.

Stein, Edith (1989) *On the Problem of Empathy*. Washington DC ICS Publications.

Stein, Edith (2002). *Finite and Eternal Being: An Attempt at an Ascent to the Meaning of Being*. Washington DC ICS Publications.

To order Fisher King Press titles call
toll free within Canada and the U.S.
1-800-228-9316
International calls
1-831-238-7799

ON THE
DOORSTEP
OF THE
CASTLE

ELIZABETH CLARK-STERN

On the Doorstep of the Castle
A play of Teresa of Avila and Alma de Leon
by Elizabeth Clark-Stern
ISBN: 9781771690027

Our setting is 16th century Spain. The Inquisition has expelled
the Jews or forced them to convert. Teresa of Avila is igniting
the imagination of the country as the nun who receives
messages directly from God. Alma de Leon, a young Jewish
converso, appears on Teresa's doorstep, petitioning to become
a novice in her care. Their complex relationship explores the
feminine archetypes of the Amazon, and the Medial Woman,
in a story that unveils the foundations of psyche's movement
toward wholeness: Kabbalah, and Christian rapture, in an
oppressive yet luminous time.

This play is a work of creative imagination based on the
interaction of a true historical character and a fictional one.

Teresa of Avila is admired to this day not only by Catholics and Christians, but by Taoists and Buddhists, psychologists and poets. Carl Jung was fascinated by her master work, The Interior Castle, for its description of the journey of the soul toward intimacy with God. The fictional character, Alma de Leon, is inspired by twentieth century Jewish philosopher, Edith Stein, who chanced to read Teresa's autobiography, and experienced a profound spiritual awakening that led her to become a Carmelite nun. "What if these two were to meet?" the playwright asked herself, crafting the character of Alma as a Jewish woman true to her time and place in history. The teaching of the ancient Jewish mystical tradition, the Kabbalah, was strictly forbidden by the Inquisition, and yet Alma is haunted by it, even as she dons the habit of a nun and struggles to find her identity in the presence of her passionate, spiritually adventurous mentor.

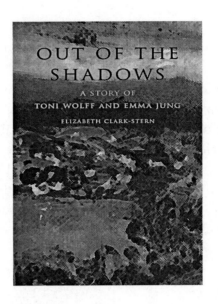

Out of the Shadows:
A Story of Toni Wolff and Emma Jung
by Elizabeth Clark-Stern
ISBN-13: 978-0981393940

The year is 1910. Sigmund Freud and his heir-apparent, Carl Jung, are changing the way we think about human nature and the mind. Twenty-two year old Toni Wolff enters the heart of this world as Jung's patient. His wife, Emma Jung, is twenty-six, a mother of four, aspiring to help her husband create the new science of psychology. Toni Wolff's fiercely curious mind, and her devotion to Jung, threaten this aspiration. Despite their passionate rivalry for Jung's mind and heart, the two women often find themselves allied. Born of aristocratic Swiss families, they are denied a university education, and long to establish themselves as analysts in their own right. Passionate and self-educated, they hunger for another intellectual woman with whom to explore the complexities of the soul, the role of women in society, and the archetypal feminine in the affairs of nations.

Their relationship spans 40 years, from pre-World War I to the dawn of the Atomic Age. Their story follows the development of the field of psychology, and the moral and professional choices of some of its major players. Ultimately, Toni and Emma discover that their individual development is informed by both their antagonism, and their common ground. They struggle to know the essence of the enemy, the other, and to claim the power and depth of their own nature.

il piccolo editions is an imprint of Fisher King Press.
Learn more about many other worthy publications at:
www.fisherkingpress.com

CPSIA information can be obtained
at www.ICGtesting.com
Printed in the USA
FFOW01n1105110614
5783FF